D1314169

Television

by Darlene R. Stille

Content Adviser: Professor Sherry L. Field, Department of Social Science Education,
College of Education, The University of Georgia

Reading Adviser: Dr. Linda D. Labbo, Department of Reading Education,
College of Education, The University of Georgia

Compass Point Books

Minneapolis, Minnesota

SAYVILLE LIBRARY

Compass Point Books
3722 West 50th Street, #115
Minneapolis, MN 55410

Visit Compass Point Books on the Internet at *www.compasspointbooks.com* or e-mail your request to *custserv@compasspointbooks.com*

Photographs ©: Gregg Andersen, cover; Unicorn Stock Photos/Tom McCarthy, 4; RDF/Visuals Unlimited, 6, 14; Unicorn Stock Photos/Jeff Greenberg, 8; Unicorn Stock Photos/Erick R. Berndt, 10; John Sohlden/Visuals Unlimited, 12; Photo Network/Tom Tracy, 16; Camerique/Archive Photos, 18; Archive Photos, 20;

Editors: E. Russell Primm and Emily J. Dolbear
Photo Researcher: Svetlana Zhurkina
Photo Selector: Phyllis Rosenberg
Designer: Melissa Voda

Library of Congress Cataloging-in-Publication Data
Stille, Darlene R.
    Television / by Darlene R. Stille.
        p. cm. — (Let's see)
    Includes bibliographical references and index.
    1. Television—Juvenile literature. [1. Television.] I. Title.
TK6640 .S82 2001
621.388—dc21   2001001452

© 2002 by Compass Point Books

All rights reserved. No part of this book may be reproduced without written permission from the publisher. The publisher takes no responsibility for the use of any of the materials or methods described in this book, nor for the products thereof.
Printed in the United States of America.

Table of Contents

What's on Television?

What's your favorite TV program? Many kinds of programs are shown on TV.

We can watch news, sports, and weather programs on TV. We can watch comedy shows and movies too.

We watch some TV programs just for fun. We watch other TV programs to learn new things.

◀ *Watching television is part of daily life for most people.*

More Than TV Shows

You can use your TV set for more than just watching TV programs. You can hook things up to your TV.

A videocassette recorder (VCR) lets you **record**, or tape, TV shows. You can play them back later. You can also rent movies on videotape to play on your VCR.

A **DVD** player lets you use your TV to watch movies recorded on digital disks. You can even hook your TV up to your computer.

Inside a TV Studio

Do you know where TV pictures come from? Many shows come from a TV studio. Some are shown **live**. Some are taped and replayed later.

Let's visit a studio. Here come the actors. They are the people you see on your TV screen.

The actors go to the set. The set is a kind of stage. Bright lights shine down on the set.

Here come the **producer** and **director**. It is their job to make sure the show goes well. They work in the control room. The control room has many dials, switches, and TV screens. Each screen shows the picture from a different TV camera.

◄ *The control room of a television studio has many screens and machines.*

TV Cameras

A sign lights up. It says the show is on the air. We must be very quiet.

The TV cameras turn on. The TV cameras capture the pictures. Microphones record the sound.

The studio uses big TV cameras on wheels. A camera operator moves each TV camera around the set.

Some TV cameras are smaller than others. TV crews use small cameras and microphones when they work outside the TV studio. TV camera crews often go to sports events and places where news is happening.

◀ *A television reporter and a camera crew go where the news is happening.*

How the Show Gets to Your House

Television systems change the pictures from TV cameras and the sound from microphones into electronic signals. The signals then go to a tower called an antenna. The antenna sends the TV signals through the air.

The signals come through the air to a TV **antenna** inside your house or on your roof. They can also come through wires from a cable TV company. They even can come from a satellite in space to a satellite dish at your house.

"Painting" a TV Picture

Your TV set turns the signals back into pictures and sounds. The TV show gets "painted" on your TV screen one line at a time. Parts inside the TV tube in the back of your TV set send out beams of TV signals.

The beams sweep back and forth across the screen. They move so fast that you cannot see it happen.

◄ *Parts inside a TV set turn a TV signal into a picture on the screen.*

Color TV Pictures

A color TV picture is formed by beams of only three colors. The colors are red, green, and blue. These three colors can be mixed together to make all kinds of colors.

See for yourself how red, green, and blue make different colors. Mix some red paint with some green paint. What color do you get? Now try mixing blue and green or red and blue.

◄ *Workers in a control room check that the colors of a TV program are correct.*

The First Televisions Sets

Television was invented in the 1920s. The first regular TV shows in the United States went on the air in the 1940s.

People watched these shows on TV sets with small screens. Some screens were round. Some TV screens were inside large wooden cabinets that sat on the floor.

The first TV sets showed only black-and-white pictures.

◄ *Early television sets showed only black-and-white pictures.*

Where TV Can Take You Now

TV cameras do more than record TV shows. Television lets you see places where you cannot go.

Astronauts take TV cameras into space. TV cameras go deep into the ocean on small submarines. Doctors use very tiny TV cameras to look inside the human body. Television keeps changing how we see the world.

◄ *Television cameras allow us to see places, such as outer space, that we could never visit.*

Glossary

antenna—a tower that sends and receives radio or TV signals

DVD (digital versatile disk)—a type of compact disk that holds much more audio, video, or text

director—a person in charge of making a TV program or movie

live—a program shown as it is happening; not taped

producer—a person in charge of presenting a TV program or a movie

record—to put sounds and images onto a tape or electronic disk to be played later

Did You Know?

• On January 13, 1928, Ernest F. W. Alexanderson showed the first television receiver that could be used in the home.

• In Boston in 1946, a major league baseball game was seen on television for the first time.

Want to Know More?

At the Library

Ganeri, Anita. *The Story of Communications*. New York: Oxford University Press Children's Books, 1998.

Oxlade, Chris. *Television*. Chicago: Heinemann Library, 2001.

Wordsworth, Louise. *Film and Television*. Austin, Tex.: Raintree Steck-Vaughn, 1998.

On the Web

How Stuff Works
http://www.howstuffworks.com/tv.htm
For a more detailed explanation of how TV works

PBS Kids
http://pbskids.org/did_you_know/lights/
For an online activity to help you learn about some of the people who make a TV show

Through the Mail

The Museum of Broadcast Communications
Chicago Cultural Center
Michigan Avenue at Washington Street
Chicago, IL 60602-4801
For more about the history of television and radio broadcasting

On the Road

The Museum of Television and Radio
25 West 52nd Street
New York, NY 10019
or
465 North Beverly Drive
Beverly Hills, CA 90210
To see exhibits on television and radio programs

Index

About the Author
**Darlene R. Stille is a science editor and writer. She has lived in
Chicago, Illinois, all her life. When she was in high school, she
fell in love with science. While attending the University of
Illinois, she discovered that she also enjoyed writing. Today she
feels fortunate to have a career that allows her to pursue both
her interests. Darlene R. Stille has written more than thirty
books for young people.**

SAYVILLE, LIBRARY
11 COLLINS AVE.
SAYVILLE, NY 11782

SEP 1 5 2003